WHO AM I?

THE JOURNAL,
PART 2
THE METAMORPHOSIS OF MY LIFE

DR. LINDA R. JORDAN

WESTBOW
PRESS®
A DIVISION OF THOMAS NELSON
& ZONDERVAN

WestBow Press books may be ordered through booksellers or by contacting:

WestBow Press
A Division of Thomas Nelson & Zondervan
1663 Liberty Drive
Bloomington, IN 47403
www.westbowpress.com
1 (866) 928-1240

ISBN: 978-1-9736-9218-8 (sc)
ISBN: 978-1-9736-9219-5 (e)

Library of Congress Control Number: 2020909225

Print information available on the last page.

WestBow Press rev. date: 5/20/2020

To Dennis. I praise God for you, Dennis, my lovely, God-fearing husband of thirty-nine years, my friend, my partner, my love, who has put up with me in all the new visions I have sought and has supported me spiritually, financially, and physically while I wrote this book. You really prove that love never fails. I love you with deep, sweet love, my honey bun.

In loving memory of my father and mother, Deacon Thomas and Deaconess Evangeline Roberson, who died in 2019. They always taught us to put God first, work hard, and use our gifts and talents while never giving up.

But, to always trust in the Lord with all your heart; and lean not unto your own understanding. And in all thy ways acknowledge him, and he will direct your path.

—Proverbs 3:5–6

CONTENTS

ACKNOWLEDGMENTS

Thank you to my sons, Dennis Jr. and Dervin, for sharing your precious time with my school schedule and for pushing me to continue school. I love you. Keep your hopes and dreams alive.

Thank you to my sisters, Angie, Mary, Faye, and Gail, my best friends forever, for supporting my book and for loving me for who I am and to my brothers-in-law, who always support a sister. You're the only brothers I have.

Blessings and thanks to Dr. Lance Watson Sr., the senior pastor of Saint Paul Baptist Church in Richmond, Virginia, for allowing the fact finding of my dissertation to become a part of and a support for developing small groups for teenage girls, young ladies, and the women's ministry workshops under Barnabas Counseling Ministries as an ordained minister, servant leader, and member; Dr. Sonia Banks.,Overseer for Barnabas Counseling Ministry small group, St. Paul Baptist

Richmond Va, for the Push to start small group for teen girls, and young ladies, Dr's. Virgil and Mary Winters, pastors, mentors, friends, and family at Plentiful Harvest Ministries in Richmond Va; Reverend Philip Knight, father -in- ministry and Pastor at Rockhill Baptist in Hanover, Virginia; Pastor Gerald and Dorothy Fountain at Rejoice Christian Center, my mentors and friends; Apostle Ed. Montgomery and Bishop Cassandra Montgomery PHD, my Spiritual Adviser and Mentor, of the Family Bible Ministry Worldwide Seminary University in Towson, Maryland. Thanks for your guidance, leadership, instruction, direction, and encouragement with much nurturing love.

Special thanks to Dionne M. Hughes, author, friend, and owner of the Image Enhancement Center. Thank you for the love you gave in mentoring as a leader to me while on your team, which inspired me to dream, believe, and finish my book.

Thanks to Dorothy Fountain and Nancy Brown, my special friends, for proofreading this book. I love you so much.

Thanks to all who have helped and encouraged me along the way.

STAGE 1

THE EGG

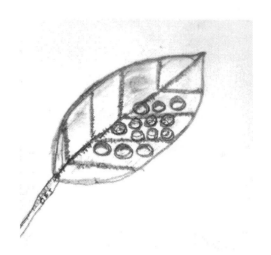

A while back I spoke to a group about the metamorphosis of a butterfly and how much I had learned from my research. Little did I know that it was about me—my past, present, and future. In that session I spoke on transformation, transforming, and change of form. I knew that the word that was spoken on that day was an unveiling and cleansing for the group members as well as myself.

The beginning of the metamorphosis process is not so beautiful, because it begins with gross-looking, slimy, yellowish-green eggs, and so was my past as a fresh, green teenager on a date with an older boy. He seemed young enough to me, but he was too old according to my parents. But what young person cares about age when she *thinks* she is in love. My parents wanted to know everything, all the information they could get from us girls, about the guys we liked as friends or had a more serious interest in.

As a teen girl, I felt that the information my parents sought wasn't important. My business was my business. Not sharing with the most important people in my life could have caused a problem later. Some teens may think that parents are nosy, but when it comes to protecting a girl's best interest, her heart, emotions, and future, the nosiness of parents is a good thing.

My heart needed all the guarding and protecting until I could learn to guard it on my own with the help of God. I didn't have time for that kind of mentoring and teaching. I was a quick, fast, and in-a-hurry kind of girl. I wanted what I wanted, and I wanted this dating thing to work out for me.

I was at the first stage of the metamorphosis part of my life, the egg. I was new to the reality of the dating world. I was looking for love in all the wrong places or people. You would have thought that I didn't have a lovely father and mother who shared their love in such a caring atmosphere in our home. My mother was a prayerful Christian woman, an example of how to keep a home and be a loving wife. Dad was a man of great standards with a compassionate and nurturing heart for his girls. We went on walks with him, and he told us stories of life and stories his parents had told him and his brothers and sisters. My favorite was about all the animals that helped the pig jump over the fence to get home late one night.

Dad disciplined us with the Word of God and by the wisdom given to him, I believe, by God. Mom did more spanking. Dad was more reserved, which was a great balance. I started as a high school student who went after what I wanted. You could say I was an outgoing busybody. Having a boyfriend was very important to me. Dad and Mom always encouraged us to wait and allow the guy to find us and to never go looking for a guy. Well, that advice must have been for my sisters—surely not for me. I had convinced myself that I knew a lot about a lot.

My date was just a bit older than I was. I thought he was nice and handsome, and he had a positive image. That worked for me. I didn't look for him. He was in my view, and I told someone that I liked him and thought he was cute. My friend didn't keep my secret for long, and so really, he didn't find me—I found him.

I now had a new friend and date; I was hoping that we could plan a future for ourselves, college or even a family. I was very serious about this dating thing, even as a young girl.

I always wanted to go to the movies, and so when he asked me, I said yes. I thought, *What a nice guy! He's taking me to the movies, and maybe we'll get some popcorn. Wait until I tell my friends.* Selling yourself short is not healthy for your self-esteem. You can buy your own popcorn and movie ticket. You can take your time, not be anxious about anything. You are talking about your life, your worth, your life's value, and the royalty of your life in God's eyes.

During the date, I started to have a feeling inside like an upset stomach with butterflies in it. I should have gone with the way I was feeling, but my pride dictated that he was going to take me to the movies and all. Besides, what would my friends have thought if I had backed out and asked him to take me home because of some little old butterflies?

Always go with what you feel deep inside. It was a great warning. Well, the date was a disappointment. It was one of the worst nights I could ever imagine, my emotion was out of control and my expectations were far from met. It was too late to implement my parents' guidance and advice—maybe on my next date.

The heart is very fragile. You can't allow anything and everything to come in and out of your heart. You must guard it with all your might. You can let God protect you—he can even use your parents.

I didn't know much about releasing anger or letting it go, and I guess I knew very little about life, people, guys, girlfriends, and relationships after all. This became my caterpillar stage of life. I was outraged and didn't trust many people or guys.

Now journal your thoughts: "I knew you" (Jeremiah 29:1).

_____

_____

_____

_____

_____

_____

_____

_____

_____

_____

_____

_____

_____

STAGE 2

THE CATERPILLAR

This is when emotionally I started to gather all types of issues, good and bad. I survived the shocks in my life and even lived through the drama of high school. This took me to the second stage of metamorphosis, the caterpillar. I was emotionally eating by holding onto everything I could find and blame for the way I was feeling about myself. I never knew it was an issue within, but I knew that no one was ever going to betray me again. I started to guard my own heart and didn't trust anyone much, especially men.

I had become a young woman in college with some life experience and a little more knowledge of how the guy-girl dating situation goes. Scorched from my past and afraid of the future, college was wonderful and fun, and shopping on lunch breaks was even more fun. I thought college was only for socializing, and maybe a little class work.

I made a few new friends, girls and guys, and even started dating again. One of my sister's old friends introduced me to the love of my life. I could not tell that he was my future husband. He was too young for me; he looked like a little boy, and I didn't like immature guys. I told him that I would go on a date with him. I wanted to see if it might work out, and it turned out great because he was an old soul. I couldn't tell that he was only two years older than I was.

He was very handsome with the most beautiful eyes. This got my attention, but I didn't let him know. I tried to focus on getting to know his plans for the future and whether God came first in his life. He answered yes to my question about God in his life. He had just started working for the airlines, and I was impressed. I then explained my plans for my future. We kept dating as I continued college, and all the while I was falling in love with him.

Things were going well, and then the unthinkable happened. I became pregnant, and we had to make some decisions and new plans for our future. I was living with my oldest sister, and my lifestyle was about to change. We ultimately decided to get married because it was right for the baby. By that time, I was six months pregnant and could not bear the thought of being abandoned by the one I loved, and trust was already an issue. Poor thing! He didn't know what he was getting into! He was getting a baby and a scorned, outraged girl for a wife, one who brought hidden concerns into the relationship— concerns that she had not dealt with.

I gave birth to a son at the age of nineteen and named him after my twenty-one-year-old husband. He was new, the baby was new, and our life was new—we were very green. It all happened at once, and it was a bit too much for me.

I was now a mother whose only plans were to raise a child and be a wife because all my other plans—to model, work in the fashion industry, get into acting and maybe dancing— had gone out the window. It was over. I had to go to work somewhere to help pay for a babysitter and bills. This wasn't what I had planned, but my child was here. I wanted to be a mom, but what about me? It wasn't about me anymore—it was about my little family, and so I had to make new plans.

Family is important. My parents always made us feel special and important, and I recognized that I had to do the same for my new family.

Five years later, we had another child. I was twenty-four, and my husband was twenty-six. We were growing into a nice-looking family but without the picket fence. I started to express more distrust and jealousy, and I cried out for more attention from him. Surely he was wondering what he had gotten himself into. My temperament and my learned behavior from my past experiences were really showing. We all must learn where we are in the stages of our lives.

Consider the following questions:

1. How does this relate to you?
2. Are you in this stage of your life?
3. A relationship with God is the first step toward forgiveness and healing in your life. Start with Romans 10:9–10. Read, and receive him into your heart.

4. The second step starts when you ask God to forgive the person who hurt you.

5. Now ask God to heal your heart. Remember that this is a process toward healing each day.

Now journal your thoughts: "You created my innermost being" (Psalm 139:13–14).

_____

_____

_____

_____

_____

_____

_____

_____

_____

_____

_____

_____

STAGE 3

THE COCOON

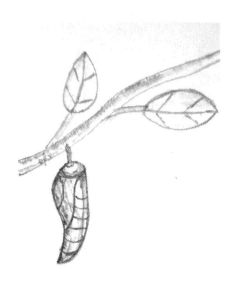

I became insecure in our marriage. Both the cocoon and the caterpillar stages are very sensitive. In the cocoon stage, I had to process and illuminate. I needed answers to some of my daily thoughts. I even thought about taking my own life. I didn't like myself or my life because hurt and pain were leading my emotions.

This caused problems with how I communicated my thoughts with other people, including my husband. I threw objects, anything I could find to break, and didn't talk at all about what was really wrong or what caused my outrage. My husband would ask, "What's wrong with you? Are you crazy? At the same time, I blamed my husband for it all. He was the man of the house, and he was supposed to fix what was wrong. But he couldn't fix me. I knew that I had issues, and while I wasn't crazy yet, I did know that if I kept going into rages, I would soon be heading there or even prison or death.

I was still going to church and taking my sons at times. I felt that I was listening to God every now and then, and I thought maybe that was where I needed to start getting help. Outrage isn't a good thing. It meant something was going on inside that was not good for me or my family. I tried listening more to God and getting more involved in the ministry, even singing in our family group. My attitude started to change, and there was less outrage.

While visiting other ministries, I knew I needed to get closer to God. I needed to study his Word. I started going to Bible study at a local charismatic ministry. I grew in my gifts and in my knowledge of who God is. A few years later, I felt led by God to attend Bible school, and I drew even closer to him. I even started to forgive my past dates.

I read in the Bible that while Jesus was on the cross, he asked God to forgive his killers for they knew not what they did. Jesus had already forgiven them for the way they treated him. I repeated this scripture and believed that it would work for me as well.

I was no longer angry with my past date. I asked God to have mercy on him and to save his soul. As I continue to study the Word of God, I found myself and noticed that Psalm 139:13–14 stated that I was made by God, that he knit me together in my mother's womb, and that I am fearfully and wonderfully made in his image. His work is wonderful. I was not so bad after all. I was made in the image of God, and he made me beautiful inside and outside. No person can determine who I am—only God can because he made me. And he loves me.

Shortly after finishing the first year in Bible school, I accepted the call into the ministry and continued growing in my attitude and emotional healing day by day.

Consider the following:

1. What is happening in your life? Are you in this stage of your life?

2. Is it time to move forward to the next stage of your life?

3. Read Psalm 139:13–14 to assure yourself of who God says you are.

4. Now forgive yourself for blaming and holding yourself accountable for your encounters or adverse experiences.

Now journal your thoughts:

_____

_____

_____

_____

_____

_____

_____

_____

_____

_____

_____

_____

STAGE 4

THE BUTTERFLY

The butterfly is the final stage of metamorphosis. At this stage inside a pupa, a miracle happens, and from the cocoon emerges a butterfly.

I was in the butterfly stage of my life. I graduated from Faith Landmark Bible Institute in Richmond, Virginia, and was licensed as a minister three years later. To me it meant preparation before the assignment from God—Jesus did a lot of things in threes. I continued to grow and commuted to Seminary University in Towson, Maryland. It was a sacrifice, but God prevailed because there was something special there for me and my family.

While learning the Bible's history, exegeses of scriptures, and all about personality types and temperaments, I learned more about me and who I am in my class called Creation Therapy. This was the beginning of a real breakthrough in knowing who I am. There were counseling classes based on inborn temperament, meaning the personality type God had given me when he created me. I learned how they operated in my life and how to balance my temperament in my everyday life, and I learned to control controlling my life as I balanced my strength and strengthened my weaknesses. A miracle was about to happen to me while in this stage, just like a butterfly emerging from the cocoon.

I had completed all the phases of counseling in seminary, had earned a master's in counseling, and was continuing with my doctoral coursework. A dissertation was required for completion of my degree, and the only subjects that were magnified before me were about family relationships, how to communicate on the job, how to find a career that suits your temperament, and marriage communications. No one really understands who they are or who the other person is. If there is pain, why we can't communicate the pain inside? How can they stop the pains?

While traveling to the mountains in Charlottesville, Virginia, to find the answer about who I am and my temperament type research, I not only found out about myself but also about my husband. God showed his personality to me and let me understand how my husband sees things in life. God revealed to me that I should stop trying to change him into what I desired him to be and being offended by him and that I should free my heart from being so sensitive to past hurt and pain.

I needed to focus on myself and how to balance my temperament. The more I learned about temperament, the better I could communicate some of the things I wanted to express to my husband without rage or running away from disagreement or staying angry with him for a long period of time. Trying to understand one another was an ongoing, everyday process, but we made it to the final stage of metamorphosis and became butterflies.

Like a butterfly, I could go as far as my dreams would take me according to God's plans for my life as I endured this incredible change of being healed, delivered, and becoming a butterfly. My life is not my own, and that's why I decided to share my life's story and the tools of my awareness.

Consider the following:

1. Is this where you are now in your life?
2. After reading this chapter, how can you get here?
3. Read 2 Corinthians 5–17: new creation in Christ, all things are passed away, and all things become new.
4. Read Jeremiah 29:11, God's plan for you.
5. Prayer of confession. Meditate on prayer.

Now journal your thoughts:

_____

_____

_____

_____

_____

_____

_____

_____

_____

_____

_____

_____

_____

CONFESSIONAL PRAYER

Lord, I praise you because you are our Creator, for Psalm 139:13–14 says that you knit me together in my mother's womb and that I am fearfully and wonderfully made. I believe you made me and I am not a mistake because you knew that I was coming into this world.

I now come against the spirit of confusion inside of me about who I am. You are the great I Am, and you are the beginning and the end of my life. You are the head and not the tail. You are above and not beneath. My spirit is alive, not dead, because I welcome you, Jesus, into my life. Jesus, please breathe life into me. I praise you today for who you are in me. Please live in me. Thank you, Lord, for creating me. I love you, Lord, and I love me, for I am created in your image.

In Jesus's name, amen.

If you believe this and would like to walk in freedom from depression, darkness, fear, hate, and sadness and be closer to

Jesus Christ, Romans 10:9–10 says that if you declare with your mouth that Jesus is Lord and believe in your heart that God raised Jesus from the dead, you will be saved.

Lord, I believe that you are Lord. Forgive me for all my sins. I receive you into my heart today, and I thank you for healing me. In Jesus's name, amen.

REFLECTION

God placed me in a class called Creation Therapy, based on Psalm 139:13–14 God created our innermost being, spirit, heart, and emotions. He knit us together in our mothers' wombs. We praise God, for we are fearfully and wonderfully made. God's work is wonderful. He made me. I am not a mistake but wonderfully made. I know this full well, and I do believe that he is my Creator. I know who I am in Christ. I no longer need people to affirm who I am because I know who God says I am, and since I received him into my life, I am now a new creature in Christ. That's who I am.

My 2003 doctoral dissertation became the basis for this book. I praise God for his wisdom, for he sees the bigger picture. He is an all-knowing God in everything in our life.

BIBLIOGRAPHY

Arnos Profile, Creation Therapy, Biblically Based Christian Counseling, Richard Gene Arno,PH.D, Author, Phyllis Jean Arno, PH.D Co-Author Copyright 1996 Sarasota Fl. All Rights Reserved (NCCA) National Christian Counselors Association

WWW.earth life.net Gordon's 1st Lepidoptera

Printed in the United States
By Bookmasters